Hopefully This Helps

Michael Sean Irgang

Copyright © 2023 by – Michael Sean Irgang

All Rights Reserved.

It is not legal to reproduce, duplicate, or transmit any part of this document in either electronic means or printed format. Recording of this publication is strictly prohibited.

Dedication

To everyone fighting the good fight.

@hopefully_this_helps

The only true calling I've ever personally felt in my life is to help people feel better in my short time interacting with them. To take their mind off of whatever bullshit is getting to them and physically be present with them. My honest belief is that people are here to peacefully exist and assist one another in their everyday lives. Unfortunately, that's just not how the world works. I believe there is so much more to life and it's extremely easy to drown in the sorrows from all of our negative experiences. This is just my personal collection of views, tips, isms, excuses, and my brain's overall take on the world. These are in no specific order, as are the things that life throws at you. Peace be with you and your loved ones. You either get it or you don't.

- You can always learn how to do something. Just as importantly, make sure you also learn how not to do things. It was the latter for me.

- It's okay to have high standards. It's not okay to be a perfectionist.

- Please use your turn signal. It's free and comes standard with every car.

- You can only go wait at a bus stop so many times before you realize the bus isn't coming.

- Feel free to move wherever you'd like geographically, but always know you can never move from the space in between your ears.

- Patience really is a virtue.

- Share and express your love for others.

- It's all bullshit.

- Use your manners. Please and thank you go a long way, try it.

- Everyone has an opinion, and everyone is right in their minds.

- I know highly educated people who make dog ass daily decisions.

- Americans are shitty. You're probably an American.

- Wash your hands after using the restroom, with soap.

- Be realistic, not everything can be accomplished at once.

- My personal goal is to be 1% better each day; it adds up real quick.

- It's not hard to be genuine.

- We can justify anything we want in our minds. It's still wholesome to do the right thing.

- Dream of a better place and a better time; work towards it.

- You literally have a choice in everything, think about it.

- People will justify anything. Mentally, you have to.

- It's totally okay not to like small talk with people.

- Learn to have a filter. It's simple maturity.

- Use your brain for the better, please.

- In my opinion, yours sucks.

- Someone else's poor coping skills are not your problem (your poor coping skills are not my problem).

- I smiled pretty big when I realized everything is wrong. I smiled even bigger when I accepted it.

- If I see you on the ground, I'll reach out to help you. If you're content, I'll keep moving.

- Can't fix stupid; can't fix shit really.

- There's always three sides; your side, my side, and the truth.

- There is a difference between having free time and being available.

- Love is the most powerful thing in this universe.

- I don't let shitty people in my house.

- There is such a thing as second chances. There is also such a thing as learning from the past.

- Many times people will talk if/when they feel uncomfortable…don't feel the need to entertain or participate in these discussions.

- Believe what you want but please make sure it's not complete bullshit.

- Sometimes the more people talk the less I want to hear.

- You know you're in the presence of something special when it actually all makes sense.

- Life makes sense. Then it doesn't. Repeat.

- If you're going to do something, anything, do it confidently.

- You're never wrong for feeling a certain way; you're only wrong if you don't talk about it.

- Some people need to know it's not their problem to solve.

- You have to be very smart to be that sad.

- Addressing something doesn't make you an asshole; those who avoid it will call you one.

- People would rather defend their initial opinion rather than actually listen to the message and learn.

- There's always a way if you take the initiative.

- Communication is absolutely key.

- Silence can answer many things at times.

- You're not going crazy; you're just realizing there wasn't much order to begin with.

- We live in a country that preaches wanting better for the next generations; yet all I've seen is ridicule when that step is taken.

- The moment you realize you don't have to react any sort of way to anything, you are in control.

- There are people who would rather complain about being stuck behind a semi-truck instead of making a lane change; if you don't even check your mirrors, I have no sympathy for you.

- Being direct is really hard for people lately; apparently so is being polite.

- People are screaming because nobody is actually listening to them; you hear what you want, not what they're communicating.

- Prioritizing yourself isn't being selfish and those who fail to realize that are probably draining you the most.

- It's okay to admit you're not the best at something or that you don't know. Actually it's quite proper.

- Don't fall victim to, "the next chapter will be better". The future is only in your mind, you will only ever be living in this exact moment.

- If something's not working, change something.

- There are people who would rather complain about being stuck behind a semi-trick instead of making a lane change; if you don't even check your mirrors I have no sympathy for you.

- Tell the truth.

- Lots of humans hate being accountable.

- Not everyone wants to hear it.

- There's a difference between letting someone walk all over you, and choosing not to speak with someone who won't listen.

- Practice caring for your people.

- A lot of people who say the grass is always greener don't even water their own lawn.

- One way to minimize anxiety is to trust others; you don't always have to have things calculated. Sometimes you are a part of something bigger and need to be present in the moment to enjoy it.

- The more concerned you are with others, the less of yourself you are.

- Don't be a douchebag.

- Many people will freely give you bad advice.

- Stick around messy people long enough and you'll be dirty, too.

- If it looks like a duck, walks like a duck, and quacks like a duck, don't let anyone tell you it's not a fucking duck.

- People are bad at taking hints. Just be blunt and spell it out.

- I'd love to stay and chat, but I don't.

- There's a difference between being direct, and being confrontational.

- Hold the door open for others. Holding the door open for others is one of the simplest ways to acknowledge someone's presence. It can honestly change someone's day. But don't wait too long either, there's definitely an appropriate distance you can just let yourself in and they'll get the door for themselves.

- It's loud in my brain, too.

- There are two concrete facts about every human being: humans are creatures of habit, and, all behaviors are learned in some fashion.

- If you don't squeeze every last bit of life out of your toothpaste, we're not the same. Also, if you squeeze from the middle, you're an animal.

- Never stop learning; other's mistakes are literally a free lesson in life for you.

- Highly recommend keeping your work and personal life separate.

- When it comes to sink or swim, if you're on the team, we'll always teach you to swim, or at least tread water.

- Don't stand in doorways. There's no analogy here; don't block high traffic areas.

- Your heart is never wrong. Your mind plays tricks though.

- Unless you ask a person directly, the only narrative you have is with yourself. That's pretty one-sided if you ask me.

- Americans, as individuals, are the number one people who think they are the exception to rules.

- Not everyone is well rehearsed in dealing with their emotions.

- Humans are pretty cool when they're not total pieces of shit.

- Liars are the worst people to deal with because there's no common reality.

- Don't talk to those who won't listen; maybe they will eventually, but that's not on you.

- If you want to find the easiest way to do something, find the laziest man. Hearing this was like a slap in the face for me, thanks Rose.

- Learn to be a lifelong learner. You can learn something from everyone.

- Respect those in authoritative positions who can make decisions, especially when you're not in a situation to decide anything.

- If you honestly wouldn't speak it in front of someone, don't speak it behind them.

- You'd rather have more than not enough, of anything.

- The difference is choosing to complain or choosing to take action.

- There's plenty of smart, dumb people; there's plenty of dumb, smart people.

- The difference between knowledge and wisdom is purpose.

- A lot of people talk when they get anxious (talking is a form of self-soothing, humans do this when they're uncomfortable). You don't always have to say something, even if it's because the room is quite.

- Don't insert yourself in someone's life and then get upset if they have a reaction you don't like about it. Regardless of your intentions, you weren't asked for help.

- Sometimes all a person needs is to be listened to and validated, some people aren't always looking for answers as much as they want to be felt.

- Some people have a hard time just being present with others, but that's all my life goal is.

- Cool. That doesn't answer my question though.

- If you find you keep getting "less than" responses from someone, stop going to them.

- There's definitely a structure to life. Not everyone thinks so, which is fine, but you'll notice a difference in who believes what.

- Victimization is a manipulation tactic used by people who feel they can never do any wrong.

- The worst answers you'll ever get will be the ones you give yourself because you never actually asked the question to someone in the first place.

- Life's crazy, love isn't.

- Just keep rolling with the punches; half of them don't even land anyways.

- Not everyone is well rehearsed with their words.

- Continuous band-aids don't fix bleeding arteries.

- You'll never learn to fly if you don't try (Sledz).

- Chances are you're already more in tune with human emotions than the person calling you, "over-dramatic/emotional".

- It's not up to you to decide how someone else should go about doing anything.

- Not everyone sees the world the way you do, but it's amazing when you find people who do.

- I will never say, "I love you" to someone I don't respect. Good looks Shauny.

- Actions will forever be greater than words.

- The more a person uses "I" or "me" in conversations, the less I want anything to do with them.

- You definitely have two ears and one mouth for a reason. Use your brain more.

- Get comfortable being uncomfortable.

- No pressure, no diamonds.

- There is a difference between opinion and fact even though not many people speak like it.

- You can discredit opinions, not emotions.

- Don't force anything, there's a trick to everything.

- Inserting yourself and wanting to do it your way is not how you meet someone where they're at, regardless of your intentions.

- Adults are just grown up teenagers; some eventually mature.

- Speak with as little opinion as possible in your voice.

- Our society doesn't value inward reflection. We're designed to look outward; produce, sell, and buy things for our pleasure and happiness (I always loved working with you Lindsey).

- When expressing your ideas to others, don't start with, "you should".

- Pay attention to your tone when you speak.

- Accountability, is the difference.

- Sometimes people are just too proud to apologize and will give you anything else except.

- I'm not crazy, you just can't keep up with me.

- Take a nap.

- Everyone's just trying to get their cut.

- Seriously, though, sleep if you're tired. It's a very underrated coping mechanism but it allows your brain and body the recharge it needs.

- Try again tomorrow.

- There is so much unscripted humor all around you; stop fighting it.

- The same people who have difficulty in dialogue are the same ones who never learned to fully listen.

- Being blatantly honest can really bother people, but the truth shouldn't bother anyone.

- You can demonstrate respect to people you don't like. It's actually called 'being civil'.

- Play the game. The social game.

- Being coworkers doesn't make you friends.

- Ask questions. Ask all kinds of questions.

- Even failing is a learning experience (hit 'em Sledz).

- Learn to prioritize, well.

- Can't get mad at someone who's trying without any direction; but nobody wants to give direction, and nobody wants to listen.

- Don't name call, especially in arguments. All logical dialogue is lost afterwards.

- Behaviors are simple to understand.

- Please don't be the person who asks, "what do you do for work?" in small talk. Instead, you can ask, "what do you like to do for fun?"

- Meet people where they are at in their life, and then care for them as fit.

- Love is the answer.

- Your body can't keep up with your thoughts.

- There are rules; as in life. There is a standard. You don't always need to be vanilla, but don't lose touch with reality either.

- If you fart and it smells good, enjoy it. If not, excuse me.

- You really don't realize how much I actually filter myself.

- If you don't like home cooking, learn to cook better, with seasoning.

- There is such a thing as good tasting ice (it most likely comes from a gas station). I personally like the clear cubes the best, others prefer the pellets, chips, or even the big cylindrical ones with holes in the center; all totally delicious. But not from your fridge at home.

- Stop acting like people don't hear you; they're just smart enough to be quiet and let you keep talking.

- There is a method to the madness; or at least there should be.

- You can tell me anything you want, but I'm going to watch what you do.

- Life's full of shitty people. Don't be one of them.

- Don't push someone into a corner and judge them when they react; likewise, look in a mirror every once in a while.

- You don't always need to respond (especially with words).

- Everything with limitations.

- Don't let anyone complicate something so simple for you.

- You're not gonna like it but I'll be there.

- Own up, apologize, learn.

- Approaches matter.

- Be polite everyone.

- People can be nice outwardly, it's their inner thoughts and viewpoints you have to be wary of. I know lots of nice people at face value with super shitty opinions but it doesn't really mean I call them for coffee.

- Politics can be a really tough subject.

- Listen to your heart, ask questions if you need.

- Reflect on your personal efforts before complaining.

- Do not accept anything you are not satisfied with, especially answers from other people.

- Anxiety is worrying about the future, trauma comes from our past, depression is feeling defeated. There are very strong emotions attached to each of them, very strong. It's okay to experience them, it's not okay to hide from them.

- People literally pick and choose the information they want to take as fact; be as accurate as you can be.

- Your intentions can be misinterpreted via poor communication.

- In every instance there is a universal truth, with a million interpretations.

- There are good people out there. There's a ton of shitty people, but I promise there are decent one's too.

- "It's time to be grown up" doesn't mean 24/7, but make sure to pay your bills on time.

- Pretending like something doesn't exist is the wrong way to handle anything. Something is obviously there.

- People love to think they can multitask well.

- You'd think people can take the hint, sometimes you just need to spell it out though.

- Me choosing not to make small talk with people doesn't mean I'm shy, nor does it make it an open invitation to come chat with me. I promise you I was content.

- Hang out in the kitchen at parties. Don't eat up their house, but I promise it's where the most traffic, interactions, and enjoyment will be.

- If you find yourself in a relationship with someone constantly trying to "out polite" or "not bother" them, use clear and direct communication (e.g. I'm going to, I need to…by all means, STOP ASKING QUESTIONS).

- All the people you admire deal with the same thing you do, it's just with different idiots (love my sister for this one).

- Your freedom of speech does not excuse you from the emotions you incite from others. The minute you speak, you directly affect others. Feeling free to say what you want without thinking it will affect others is just crazy.

- When I hear the "Freedom of Speech" argument it's almost like a personal caveat for people to bully or discriminate others.

- If you're going to argue, stick to the points and use accurate facts.

- Perspective is everything, and yours isn't the only seat in the house.

- People are visual, so paint a picture for them.

- Learn from your mistakes.

- Practice verbalizing.

- If you've made it this far, you're one of the people who continues to make this world go 'round.

- If you don't feel like talking to someone, don't.

- Pay attention.

- It's not, "they have to be held responsible" …that's actually what "accountability" is. You're really trying to say, "they have to be held accountable" to the person who's responsible.

- The difference between one side of the tracks and the other is those who commit to a belief for other like-minded beings; it's the difference between a true community and individuals living for themselves.

- Before you talk about facts, be sure it is.

- Not everyone is here to be your friend, you don't even want to be friends with a majority of people truthfully.

- Don't throw people under the bus; don't be the bus driver either.

- Only speak on your behalf and what you can truthfully attest to.

- Have a place for everything, there's a place for everything.

- Learning and efficiency go hand in hand.

- When it rains, it pours.

- Pick and choose your own headaches. (this one's about prioritizing efforts; not the same as saying don't address the issue).

- You don't have to be friends with everyone.

- Make sure you have a good umbrella.

- If an adult hasn't learned accountability, their child won't either.

- Your intentions might not be what someone else wants right now.

- Some people really need things spelled out for them.

- Focus on doing one thing, really well, at a time.

- You'd always rather have more and not need it than not have enough to begin with.

- I whole heartedly believe people are here for one another, even though social interactions don't reinforce this all the time, don't let other people blind you from your love.

- Don't make someone feel guilty for something you could've done yourself; lazy.

- Be very wary of people's manipulation tactics; they'll have you feeling shitty and you did nothing wrong, you probably didn't even do anything.

- Use your sick/personal/vacation days. Your business will replace you tomorrow if you died today. It's not personal, and neither is using your time how you'd like.

- If you think about it, the truth is super logical.

- Not everyone is going to share your sense of humor.

- Sorry if I'm late everyone, I shit my pants.

- If both sides are pointing the finger at each other, who's working on solutions?

- Speak as logical as you can, and please make sure it makes sense.

- Human behavior can be summed up to two things: to obtain, to avoid.

- Interrupt your anxious/nervous thoughts with, "what if everything goes right?".

- Don't talk out of your ass, just be honest and say, "I don't know, I'm not sure".

- Love makes the world go 'round.

- Nike Crocs.

- It's pretty apparent to others when your priorities are not in order.

- Mirrors exist for a reason but a lot of people don't like to look in them; stop blaming everyone else for your problems.

- The most difficult thing for humans to do is admit their own fault. It's almost comical at times.

- If your priority in dialogue is to defend your ego, you're off track.

- Many people will give you answers you didn't even ask questions about.

- My butt's leaking, I don't know what to tell you.

- For some reason people feel super free to give their opinion on how things "should" be.

- It's not enjoyable to be around people who complain all the time; tell them that.

- You can prove people right, or you can prove people wrong.

- Don't hope it will be better, make it better.

- Your maturity level can be demonstrated in how you problem solve.

- In grieving, everyone is hurting. Do your best to be thoughtful.

- You don't need to respect other's opinions, but you do need to respect their emotions and the fact they're only human, too.

○ All animals are equipped with a "Fight-or-Flight" response. This instinctive response provides the body with a great deal of adrenaline in order to move at peak physical performance. Blood vessels widen, your heart pumps faster, your eye sight broadens, etc. Most of the time this kicks in when there is an immediate threat or danger to us or our environment. The thing about humans, though, is that this response can be initiated purely by thought alone, without any physical reinforcement saying we are actually in danger (this is anxiety/depression in a nutshell). So when this happens, take a long deep breath and look around the room, because if there isn't something immediately threatening you (like being in a room with a lion face to face) then you need to focus on regulating your body; starting with your thoughts and mind. Your problem hasn't disappeared, but at least your body and mind are more prepared to handle the situation.

- You can never go wrong if you stick to true facts and genuine logic.

- Just because I'm quiet doesn't mean I don't have something to say, I just don't care enough to share it with you, or simply don't want to.

- I really don't care but professionally I feel like I should bring this up.

- Prioritize your priorities.

- I'll always support you, but I can't support toxicity.

- Play is the universal form of communication; toddlers, kids, adults, everyone understands play in some fashion.

- Don't over do it.

- Not everyone has something "beneficial" to teach you, but hopefully you learned something.

- Everyone wants to help complete the puzzle, but sometimes the puzzle piece others bring around is to an entirely different puzzle.

- There's a lid for every pot.

- The people who are first to judge and last to listen will always tell you how things should be.

- The halt of progression lies within upholding shitty opinions.

The World We Live In

The world we live in
can seem real strange.
With so many people
resistant to change.
Opinions and facts
are often intertwined,
It's hard to decipher
what's in between the lines.
The world we live in isn't going right.
There's too many people
who are willing to fight.
And violence isn't the answer,
I'm sure you will see.
Because peace is the way,
wouldn't you agree?
The world we live in has many people fooled.
The media sure doesn't help,
haven't you been schooled?
Speaking of which,
they shove academics straight down your throat.
Meanwhile plenty are left
without emotional hope.
This is the problem,
in the world you see,
humans are not robots,
we're not machines.
Yet we punch in and punch out
just to feed this disease.
The world we live in doesn't seem to value individuals.
But I do.
I love you.

The End

www.ingramcontent.com/pod-product-compliance
Lightning Source LLC
LaVergne TN
LVHW061041070526
838201LV00073B/5134